IPHONE

USER MANUAL

FOR **NEWCOMERS**

All in one iOS 12 guide for beginners and seniors (iPhone, 8, X, XS & XS Max user guide)

Stephen W. Rock

Dedicated to all my readers

Acknowledgement

Ii want to say a very big thank you to Michael Lime, a 3D builder, my colleague. He gave me moral support throughout the process of writing this book.

Table of Contents

Introduction

The title of this book already gives a hint on what the book is about. It is a guide for new users of any of the iPhone series (8/8 plus, X, XS and XS Max).

Dividing the whole book into three parts, the first part introduces you into how to explore any of the iPhone series, the middle exposes a comprehensive list of tricks and how to execute them, while the last part culminates with useful maintenance tips, including battery and overall iPhone.

Also, with the comprehensive list of commands, you'll definitely learn to be a pro in using Siri, Apple's voice assistant. You'll be a pro in using Apple Pay. You'll be an iOS 12 pro. Yes, an iOS 12 pro.

The last chapter discusses tips and tricks for Apple series 4 watch.

Now, start savoring the content of this book.

Chapter 1

Brief Summary of iPhone 8/8 Plus, X, XS & XS Max

IPhone 8

Released in September 2017, the iPhone 8 is said to be a bit bigger in size than the iPhone before it. But the difference is not as much as an experiment showed that the cases for iPhone 7 fit flawlessly.

The iPhone 8 is also said to be cased with glass at the back. This glass gives the phone about 10 grams extra weight. But we've got word that it is the most resilient glass ever. Except for the glass cover, iPhone 8 is said to have a dated design. Not much difference from the older iPhones in terms of look.

As with the screen, the bezel at the side of the display is a little bigger than the trending apple phones and it features an LCD display rather than a OLED. With the numbers, the phone reaches 5.45 x 2.65 and a screen of 4.7 inch. With a resolution of 1334 x 750 pixels.

One feature worth talking about also is the ability to enable true tone. With true tone, the screen is designed to switch look according to the lighting of the surroundings. What this does is that it makes the phones colors stay consistent. This screen of the iPhone 8 is said to be one of the best LCD displays around

The sound of the phone too is a lot better. It is said to be louder than the previous iPhone 7 with about 25%. The bass is a bit more and the overall sound of the phone is great.

While the outlook of phone at first glance might not look any different from previous models, it does pack more advanced features. Like for example, the Bionic processor is A11 chip and that makes the performance a lot faster.

Now with the camera, iPhone 8 is equipped with a f/1.8 12 megapixel camera for the back. This is capable of up to 5x zoom. The rear camera is able to shoot 4K videos at up to 60 fps. It is also capable of shooting 240fps (frames per second) for slow-mo

At the front, we have the 7 megapixel FaceTime camera that uses f/2.2 aperture and BSI sensor. There's also the option for Slow-Sync Flash. This makes lowlight photos look amazing.

As regard the battery, this one's kind of low. It's has a battery of 1821mAh. Should last you a day if used carefully. The iPhone 8 identifies with a 2GB RAM and a storage of 64GB or 256 GB

iPhone 8 Plus

iPhone 8 Plus signifies the last of the iPhones with a home button. Though we don't know what can happen In the future. But I think Apple is pretty much done with the homebutton. And even though the recent iPhone X series is the talk of town, Apple still has the iPhone 8 Plus for sale.

This phone still carries the same design as the iPhone 8 except for two basic things.

First of all the most obvious; The size. The size of the iPhone 8 Plus is 6.24 x 3.07 inches. And it features a screen of 5.5 inches. An improvement from the little brother featuring just 4.7 inches. And with big screens you should expect sharper displays. And yes it does. It comes with a display resolution of 1920 x 1080.

So with an iPhone 8 Plus, you get higher quality display than iPhone 8's 1334 x 750. It's only in the iPhone X that we see Apple moving over to OLED displays, The iPhone 8 Plus still features a LCD display. And the iPhone 8 has a PPI of only 326, the iPhone 8 Plus features a 401 PPI.

In the area of performance however, there's not much difference. Like for example they both have a Bionic chipset of A11 that's equipped with HexaCore. The RAM for iPhone 8 is 2GB while iPhone 8 Plus features higher with a storage space of up to 3GB. But that shouldn't mean a lot as RAM comes into play when you're multitasking, so unless you're a multitask guru, the extra 1GB shouldn't mean a lot.

Now the second basic difference is the camera. One features only one rear camera, the other has two. And as you've guessed it, iPhone 8 Plus slides in with double cameras. The double camera features 12 megapixels but one of them is capable of shooting with an aperture of f/1.8 wide angle lens and the other camera with f/2.8. Both with Telephoto and Optical Image Stabilization.

On the front however they're both equal as they both give a 7 megapixel sensor with f/2.2 aperture.

Still on the camera, the Plus offers an option for Portrait mode while the other does not. With Portrait mode, you be able to shoot remarkable photos and make the backgrounds blurred and add bokeh to spice up the image. Use portrait mode for all your images and you take your photo experience to a whole new level.

iPhone X

On November 3, 2017, Apple launched the iPhone X. And we're totally loving it. Its features are killer.

The iPhone X comes with a dual lens of 12 mp rear camera with a wide angle aperture lens of f/1.8 and f/24 telephoto lens. What more? It also has a front camera of a whooping 7 mega-pixel which enables you to control the exposure or use portrait mode. With its capabilities, you can now experience Augmented Reality (AR). You can use both the TrueDepth or rear camera with AR apps.

Its 7 mp TrueDepth Camera uses face ID and a superb new feature called Animoji. This transmits your facial expression through the camera and to form an animated 3D emoji. The camera is capable of recording over 5o facial muscles movements. When your face is converted to Animoji, you can use it in the messages app.

That's not all. It's all got a 10x Digital zoom, auto flash and an optical zoom. And yes, let's not forget the video capability of the phone. It's got a 4k resolution that allows you to shoot at 60 frames per second. You can also shoot slow-mo at 240 frames per second.

iPhone X also has Hexa Core which provides a better performance with the A11 Bionic chip. It's also got a 64-

bit processor that is damn so efficient with a 3GB RAM. And oh yes, it also has an ample storage of up to 64GB or 256GB. No worries about storage space anymore, right?

Now as for Battery, The iPhone X is said to have a 2716 mAh battery and is equipped with wireless charging with accessories that are Qi compatible. Though we are still expecting apple's own AirPower soon.

Regarding the screen size, it's got an OLED display of about 5.8 inches (14.73 cm). With resolution of 2436 x 1125 pixels, the iPhone X is said to be water and dust resistant, which i think is super awesome. Something also worth mentioning is that apple says when looking at the screen from an angle, users may notice a small change in color.

iPhone X also has apples new Face ID that uses the TrueDepth camera. A look at the camera and the phone engine scans the image, detecting the style and shape of your face to identify it.

iPhone XS

Launched on September 28 2018, the iPhone XS is said by some to be the perfectly sized iPhone. With 5.8 inches, it's made of excellent-quality material. A glance at the phone and there's no doubting its elegance. With iPhones, you always expect a new upgrade and iPhone XS is no different. You'll find an improvement from the iPhone X.

With the camera, you still get the same dual-camera 12mp lens with f/24 aperture. But something noteworthy is that the image sensor is larger now. Might seem like nothing but wait till you're in low light and you'll be thankful for the enormous sensor size. It's also said that that iPhone XS has a better stereo than iPhone X.

Another area in which the iPhone XS is better than iPhone X is this feature of the camera called Smart HDR. What this does is that when you hit the shutter button, it takes the picture at 3 exposures. It then blends them all together to create the perfect photo.
The reason it does this is to lighten very dark areas and darken very light areas.

There's this mind-blowing upgrade the iPhone XS also received. It's called Depth Control. What it does is it allows you to tweak the blur on a Portrait mode photo. You can increase the intensity of the blur or reduce it to any level you want.

This is really cool, who doesn't like to be able to design exactly how he wants his pictures to look like.

Let's move to battery life. It is said that the iPhone XS battery can last up to a full day. Well it's got a 2658mAh Li-ion battery which is lesser than iPhone X 2716mAh so you shouldn't expect much.
But there was a testing that showed that the screen can be kept on for 6 hours with heavy usage. Like watching videos, streaming music, using hefty apps in the background.

Well as with storage, iPhone XS still beats iPhone X. Something with apple is that they don't provide a slot for microSD. So i guess as compensation they are offering a storage space higher than iPhone X 256GB. With iPhone XS, you have option to choose between the regular 256GB or 512GB. Though you'll have to pay extra for the 512GB, i think it's worth it.

Just like its predecessor, iPhone XS comes with 2436 x 1125 pixels, Hexa Core and 64 GB storage. But hold on here comes the fun part. iPhone XS is equipped with v12.0 iOS unlike iPhone X with v11.0.1. It's got a superb 4GB RAM a lot better than iPhone X 3GB with a A12 Bionic chip unlike iPhone X A11

IPhone XS Max

It's the elephant in the room. When this guy was released in September 28, 2018, we were all blown away by the size. With a 6.5 inch display (16.51 cm), it is said to be the biggest in iPhone history. It beats the iPhone X and XS of 5.8 inches.

You might think it's great and I do too. You can now watch videos on a large screen and enjoy full display. But on the other hand, swiping from the very top of the enormous screen with one hand can be very tiring. You finally reach up to the top but then you want to hit back and you have to travel down.

With camera though, no difference. You still get the same 12mp wide (f/1.8) and telephoto (f/2.4) as iPhone XS. But in low light, the new Smart HDR and large sensor helps to reduce grain. It also gives you sweet color accuracy and bokeh.

Now of course with battery, you show expect much more. With a mAh of 3174, it's been tested to last for over 12 hours with normal usage. It's also charges faster because of the tighter coil design

It's also equipped with a A12 Bionic chip like iPhone XS unlike iPhone X A11. Unlike iPhone X iOS 11 too, It operates on iOS 12. It also has Hexa Core with 64 bit architecture and 4GB RAM

The iPhone XS Max is wrapped around with glass. Though thick, it's still prone to crash, so it's best you buy a case. Y'know, save your investment while you still can. This bad boy also has a water resistance of IP68 which is better that the previous IP67 as it can stay under water of up to 2 meters (6.6 feet) for about 30 minutes. Now that's a massive improvement from the previous 3 feet.

It's got a storage of 64GB and 256GB. And you can choose to buy the higher storage of 512GB.
As with weight, of course it should be heavier it's not big for nothing. It weighs up to 7.3 ounces lot higher than iPhone X 6.1 and XS 6.2

Chapter 2

How To Secure Your iPhone With Face ID

Setting up Face ID

Before we set anything up, let's make sure there's nothing blocking your face or the phones TrueDepth camera. Try to keep the phone with arm's length. And don't worry about contacts or glasses, Face ID can work with them.

To set it up,

1. Go to **Settings**
2. Choose **Face ID and Passcode**. Enter your passcode.
3. Select **Set up Face ID**
4. Put your phone in front of your face and hit **Get started**.
5. Make sure your face is in the frame. Move your head gently to complete the circle. When it's done, hit **Continue.**
6. You'll be asked to do it a second time. Do the same thing and click **Done.**

Using the Face ID

Tap to wake or raise to wake your phone. Hold it in portrait orientation and it should scan your face.
If you're in bright sunlight, you might want to bring the camera closer to your face.

Face ID has been tested to unlock even when you're wearing sunglasses, but not all. So if you're trying to unlock your phone but it isn't recognizing, pull the sunglass off.

How To Charge iPhone Wirelessly.

Later versions of iPhone (iPhone 8 and higher) have a glass back that enables Qi certified chargers to charge the phone wirelessly. There are many Qi certified chargers. But there are two which are Apple certified; Mophie and Belkin.

Charging wirelessly

To charge wirelessly, what you want to do is;

1. Plug your charger to the power. Be sure to use a power adapter that's recommended by the manufacturer.
2. Make sure to put your charger on a flat surface
3. Lay your iPhone in the middle of the charger with its screen facing upwards and your phone should start charging

That not all. Here are a few things to make to wireless charging run smoothly

- If vibration is turned on, your phone might very well move its position when it gets a notification as you're charging. Try to turn off vibration, at least when you charge
- Make sure your phone isn't connected to a USB when you're charging wirelessly, it won't charge.
- If your iPhone has a thick or magnetic case, remove it before charging. It might charge slowly or not at all.
- When charging, your phone might get somewhat hot. When it does, move it to a cooler environment.

Chapter 3

iPhone 8/8 Plus Tips And Tricks

Video quality like never before

Talking about video quality, iPhone 8 and 8 Plus are able to shoot rally high quality videos. You know how 1080p resolution took the world by a storm? Yeah, iPhone 8 gives you 4 times that.

That's right. They call it 4k resolution. Just imagine how sharp and vivid 4k can be. With iPhone 8 and 8 Plus you can shoot 4k at 60 frames per second.

Using 4k is actually simple, just;
1. Go to **Settings**
2. Enter **Camera**
3. Select **Record video**
4. Select **4k at 60 fps** from the options it shows

I just want you note something. When you shoot with such massive value and quality, of course the size is not going to be 20KB. It's definitely going to be heavy. And since Apple does not provide a slot for microSD, you might want to go for the option of 256GB if you know you'll be shooting more videos

Don't stop shooting

Do you remember that time when you were shooting a video and then your eyes catches an interesting image, you want to take a photo of it but you can't. You're shooting a video.

When that scenario happens with older phones, then only thing you can do is sit and watch as the awesome image goes away. But that shouldn't happen again. I mean, you have your iPhone 8. Just take the photo already.

With your iPhone 8, you can take a picture while shooting a video. Just

1. Enter **Camera**
2. Swipe over to **Video**
3. Start shooting the video
4. Look for a white circle at the corner of the screen and tap it.
5. The picture is taken and saved in **Gallery**

There's a But, though. If you take photo while shooting, you don't get the full quality as a normal camera picture.

While the snap as you shoot gets up to 3840 x 2160, the normal camera can be as clear as 4032 x 3024. But at least it's something.

Impressive format for both photo and video

We just talked about the rate at which the 4k resolution can swallow up the space of your iPhone. Yes it does but it would have been much worse if it wasn't for the new format for video and photo in the iPhone 8 and iPhone 8 Plus.

The formats are HEVC and HEIF. Standing for High Efficiency Video Coding and High Efficiency Image File respectively, what they both do is that they still allows you to take you video and photo at the same high quality but takes up smaller spaces

To start to save more space,
1. Enter **Settings**
2. Go to **Camera**
3. Then **Format**
4. Select **High Efficiency**.

Use The True Tone

This true tone is the capability of your phone to shift and change the display of your phone depending on the lighting conditions of your surroundings. It will then display colors that are steady relating to your environment.

This sweet feature was first accessible on the iPad Pro alone, but now it's open to iPhones. And iPhone 8 has it.

To turn this on or off;
1. Enter the **Settings app**
2. Move to **Display and Brightness**
3. Turn on the toggle for **true tone**

A quicker way can be to;
1. Slide and enter the **Control Center**
2. You should see the brightness slider, Long press on it
3. Turn on **true tone**

Enable Auto brightness

The auto brightness can be really helpful. IT doesn't make your phones display too low or bright. When the screens too low, you can see the contents well. And when it's to bright, it can suck away battery pretty fast.

But everyone is different some prefer to use the Auto brightness while some totally dislike it

The auto brightness has changed location on the iPhone. On the former iOS, you would have to move to Display accommodations to change Auto brightness. So if you want to turn on or off Auto brightness, here's how

1. Go to **Settings**
2. Select **Accessibility**
3. Choose **Display accommodations**.

Allow Siri know you

You know Siri, the apple assistant. Though Siri can be cold sometimes, it can be a very helpful depending on how you set it. If you let Siri to know you are, if can be able to reconnect you back to your phone in case you lose it.

That's like a Life Saver, at least your investment you have to go to waste when you lose it.

To tell Siri who you are, you have to verify that you have added yourself as a contact. After that, all you do is
1. Enter **Settings**
2. Select **Siri and Search**
3. Then **My information**

Then from the contacts you can choose your own name.

Setting Custom Ringtones

This one's a lovely feature. It enables you find out who is calling you without looking at your phone's display. How this works is that you put a particular ringtone for each person.

When Justin Bieber's tone start playing, you know it's Mark that's calling. Or if you start hearing Celine Dion's track, that'll notify you that special one is calling. It depends on if you set it like that though.

1. Go to **Contacts**
2. Choose the contacts you wish to put a ring tone for.
3. Scroll down and click **Ringtone**
4. Pick the tone you want
5. If you want to add a custom vibration, Hit **Vibration** and chose your desired vibration
6. To create your own vibration, just scroll down to the bottom.

Customize Ringtone in your iPhone 8 and iPhone 8 Plus.

Just as you're able to customize and edit so many things on your iPhone 8 and Plus, you have the ability to customize the way your control center shows up on your phone.

This is really helpful because you'll be able to remove the items that you don't use often and put the ones you really need. Like if you dont use much of Calculator, you can remove it and put something else, say Magnifier.

To do this;
1. Enter **Settings**
2. Choose **Control Center**.
3. Tap **Customize Controls**
4. If you remove a feature, hit the **red button** beside the control
5. If you add a Control, press the **green circle**.

Use The Live Photos

Live photos can be a lot of fun. It records a few seconds before you shoot a photo and after you shoot it. This enables you to store memorable moments. While photos tell a story, live photos take you in the story.

To do this;
1. Enter the **Camera**.
2. Put your camera in photo mode and ensure that **Live Photo** is turned on
3. Just hold your phone and don't move.
4. Take the photo

Use The Sprit Level

In your iPhone 8 and Plus, you have numerous features kept in it. Your iPhone has the hidden ability to work in a spirit level.

What the spirit level does is that it shows you how uneven or straight a surface is when you rest your iPhone on it. You wouldn't know because it's not a standalone app. You won't find something like **The Spirit Level App**. No, Apple stashed it away in a different app; the compass app.

So that means that to open the spirit level,
1. You have to open up the **Compass App**.
2. Slide left.
3. The spirit level should be revealed

Using Do Not Disturb

IPhone 8 and 8 plus are really great phones. And one of the things contributing to its greatness is the ability to switch to **Do Not Disturb**.

These days, people tend to get distracted when they drive and it's because of their phones. Most of the times, it's usually not their fault. They are determined not to press their phones while they drive. But then as soon as they zoom off they get a notification and they feel tempted to read it.

You can avoid that temptation by using your iPhone to the full. Use the setting called **Do not disturb**. Once you enable it, it'll silence notifications and calls.

Want to try this?
1. Head over to the **Setting**
2. Choose **Do Not Disturb**
3. You should see tree options, **Manually, Automatically, When connected to Car Bluetooth**.

When connected to Car Bluetooth can be great cause as soon as you hook up your phone to the Bluetooth, it'll switch to **Do not disturb** mode.
Automatically might not be the right choice. Your phone may end up switching to Do not disturb if you're in the

train because it determines whether you're the one driving or not by means of motion and movement.

Switch To Low Power Mode.

Just as we said, Auto brightness can help your phone not to eat much battery, but there's also another feature that does more than that. It's the **Low Power Mode** option.

If you're one who uses the phone for a long time without charging, this will really come in handy. Low Power Mode switches off the items in your iPhone that sucks battery.

Of course it'll lower the brightness. The screen also goes dark more quickly. Hey Siri is gone. Background app refresh is gone, Mail fetch gone.

All of this is to save power.
1. Enter **Settings**
2. Tap **Battery**
3. Choose **Low Power Mode**

To even make it easier, you don't have to travel to Settings. You can just add it to the control center. That is after you add it yourself

1. Move to **Settings**
2. Then **Control center**
3. Select **Customize Controls**.
4. Tap the green button next to **Low Power Mode**

41

Start Dragging And Dropping

It's no lie that dragging and dropping for apple devices were only limited to iPads. But on the iPhone 8 and Plus, you now have the power to use the drag and drop. You also have the ability to do the multi-drag option.

As the name multi-drag connotes, this is the ability for the phone to drag several applications and drop in another screen or anywhere else.

To enable this,
1. Long press on the app you want to move. If you want to move multiple, press those apps too.
2. Now drag and drop it in the place you wish
3. Don't release your hand just yet. Wait a few seconds.
4. If you drag and drop in a app, there will be folder created for the two apps

Embrace Slow Sync

If you're a photography guru, then you should have no problem understanding what Slow Sync Flash means. That's what high end cameras do. But as for we normal humans that don't use cameras every day, we can be kind of oblivious to what Slow Sync Flash is.

Slow Sync Flash is the ability of you phone to shoot at a slower shutter speed while shining the flash quickly. Most phones today shoot at a high shutter speed. And that's not a problem in bright lighting.

But when it comes to low lighting you don't want to shoot with your flash using fast shutter speed. The photo won't turn out very nice.

But with your iPhone 8 and 8 Plus you have the power of slow sync flash to use in the dark. The result; A beautiful image.

To use Slow Sync Flash, all you just need to do is use the flash to shoot.

iPhone 8's Wireless Charging

iPhone 8 and 8 Plus, the amazing phones in their glory are equipped with wireless charging. This makes way for a charging experience that's easy and effective. No more having to carry around charging cords to charge to your phone.

This is made possible because of the back of the iPhone 8 an 8 Plus which is made up of glass. This glass back uses QI certified chargers to charge the iPhone wirelessly. You can see QI certified chargers easily in stores. Especially the approved ones; Belkin and Mophie. Even Apples Airpower is underway.

To charge you phone wirelessly, just plug the charger to power then you put your iPhone on the pad as the screen faces upwards and your phone should start charging.

Rank Your Downloads

There will be many times when you wish you could just rank your downloads or prioritize them. Your iPhone 8 makes that possible with no hassle.

This will help you make the most of your iPhone 8 as it will really come in handy if you're downloading several apps. It will help you save time and download what you really need real quick.

To do this

1. Press and hold on the **Touch ID** button on your phone.
2. A menu will show now, select **Prioritize downloads** from the options.

Type Emoji Faster.

In this modern world, emojis are really taking over chats. Everybody loves them. They help express feelings in ways that texts can't.

But when typing, no one has the time to go to the emoji gallery and start looking for the emoji of choice. That just wastes time. But in your iPhone 8, you have the ability to input and add shortcuts for the emoji.

1. Go to **Settings**
2. Enter **General**
3. Then **Keyboards**
4. Select **Add new keyboard.**
5. Tap **Emoji**

Once you've added the emoji
1. Go to **Settings**
2. Then **General**
3. Select **Keyboard**
4. Choose **Add new Shortcut**

Form here you can put a word that will become an emoji. Like for example, you can input that when you type **omg**, the shocked emoji will appear.

Lock Camera Lens

When you're shooting a video on your iPhone, you want the best quality you can get from your phone. And you're iPhone 8 will give you that quality. But if you don't set it right, it can actually switch lenses and that may not be what you want.

You don't have you worry, with the new feature in iPhone 8, you have ability to lock the camera lenses without any problem.

1. Go to **Settings**
2. Select **Camera**
3. Then **Record video**
4. Toggle on **Lock Camera Lens**

Recording The Screen

In the past you would need third party apps to record screen activity. But with the iOS 11, you can record the screen with phone's inbuilt feature.

1. Enter the **Settings**
2. Select **Control Center**
3. Tap **Customize controls**
4. Press the **green button** beside **Screen Recording**

Wirelessly Transfer Data To Your iPhone 8

If you want to sell your previous iPhone or give to a friend or cousin, there's something you want to do first. You want to upgrade that phone to the latest iOS. This is because with the latest iOS, you have a feature that allows you move the contents on your old iPhone to the now one wirelessly.

You will just use the old iPhone to scan your new iPhone 8. And after you scan, you'll be asked to input your authentication code. After you authenticate, the two phones will be synced and the transfer of all your settings, contents, data should begin.

During this transfer process, your passwords too will be in unison. With this new method, you can say bye to backing up to iTunes and putting back to your new phone.

Using Portrait Lighting

This one's is a big feature. Though it's for the iPhone 8 Plus alone. They call it **Portrait Lighting**. With Portrait Lighting, you have various lighting styles from Contour Light to Stage Light to Studio Light to Natural light and more.

With Portrait lighting, there's no need for filters. It uses the information gotten on your face to give you the best of the different lighting selections.

To use this,
1. Open your **Camera**
2. Beside Photo, Select the **Portrait Mode.**
3. From here you should be able to see some circles on top of the shutter. Scroll through the options and choose your desired lighting effect.
4. Click Shutter

If you're using stage light or stage light mono, you should try to make sure that face fills up the circle as much as you can.

In portrait mode, if you don't want the blurry effect,
1. Go to **Photos**
2. Pick the image of the Portrait mode
3. Select **Edit**
4. You should see a yellow logo at the top, tap it

5. Once you tap it, the effect should be off.

Venture Into The World Of AR

AR short for Augmented Reality is an advancement in technology that fixes information on the phone into real life. It can put characters in a game on your couch right in your sitting room. Though it's digitally of course.

One of the games that you can dive into AR with is Pokemon Go. And as you've guessed it your iPhone 8 is capable of this feat

When you open the game and you point your camera at any object in the real world, the app will show what your camera sees. Then you can put a character that's around to the object. In the real world nothing is happening, it's on your phone that the action is taking place.

With AR, you don't need any special extra kit, or goggles. The wonders are all in your phone.

Use Auto Call

On your phone, the feature Emergency SOS is enabled by default already. But there's something that you haven't tried yet. It's the **Auto Call**. What **Auto Call** does is that it after you quickly click the power button five times it will automatically call the services for emergency.

But when you press five times, it won't start calling emergency immediately. A selection to call will first show up. **Touch ID** will become ineffective for a while. It's until after you put in your Passcode, that **Touch ID** can become available again.

To be able to use this feature,
1. Fire up the **Settings**
2. Select **Emergency SOS**
3. Turn on the toggle for **Auto Call**.
4. If you would like to be informed as you're calling the emergency, you can add a countdown sound.

Delete Text Easily

There will be times when you will type out mistakes, or you change your mind and want to clear out what you've written, or maybe autocorrects just made your message life more miserable. When that happens it's almost a guarantee that you will start holding down your backspace for centuries to erase the bulky texts.

But don't do that, you a have a breathtaking phone now, remember? All you do is just shake your iPhone 8 and you see an option to Undo Typing. Select that and you are able to clear all in a split second.

Okay let's say you cleared everything but then you suddenly remember that there are some important words and ideas that you want to bring back. Just do the same, shake again and select Redo.

Check Out Where You Been.

Maybe because of curiosity you want to find out what your phone usually tracks so that you will see options of locations. Or you want to find out your most visited places.

All you can do is
1. Move to **Settings**.
2. Enter **Privacy**
3. Select **Location Services**
4. Then **System services**
5. Choose **Significant Locations** or **Frequent Locations**

From here you can see the places you visit the most. IF you don't want this again, you can just turn off

Scanning Documents

You don't have to use third party apps to do this. You can do it right on your iPhone 8 with no hassle.

All you do is;
1. Enter **Notes App**
2. Make a **New note**
3. If keyboard is shown, click the **plus** button at the top of the keyboard. If keyboard is not open, look the **plus** button at the bottom of the display
4. Select **Scan Documents**
5. For an enriched scan, click the overflow icon and choose between color, grayscale or black and white

Chapter 4

Tips and tricks for the iPhone X

Shoot like a pro

If there's something we must talk about here, it's the iPhone X ability to shoot videos in high resolution.

And when I say high resolution I mean massive resolution, I mean shooting 4k resolution at 60 frames per second. As with slow motion, it's able to record 1080p at 240 frames per second . Now if you're familiar with the world of video making you'll know that's a lot.

To get to use this awesome feature;
1. Go to **Settings**
2. Choose **Camera**
3. Then **Record video**

You should see a list, choose from what it shows.

To record slow motion, look under **Camera**, a setting called **Record slo-mo** should be there.

Using the app switcher

With the iPhone X, you don't get a home button. Who needs a home button anyway when we've got new features like the app switcher.

Swipe up from the bottom of the screen like you're dong home gesture. But hold at the center of the screen. Form the left side of the screen a indicator should appear. Then you can swipe right or left.

But that kind of a long process and is used to switch to an app that was used a long time ago.

But to move through recent apps quickly, just swipe right to left or left to right from the bottom edge of the screen

Force the home button back

For diehard fans of the home button, there's a way to bring the button back. Okay you know you can't bring possibly bring back the physical home button. But that doesn't mean we are without hope.

We enable the virtual home button. Which really is a piece of cake.

1. Enter settings
2. Choose Accessibility
3. Assistive touch, you can then toggle it on

From here on, you should now see the virtual home button. You can even activate shortcuts by customizing to.

Customize Control Center

Things got way cooler with iPhone X ability to edit what appears in the control center. It really everything lot easier. You can easily reach for stuff without having to travel a long way.

To do this,
1. Enter **Settings**
2. Hit **Control Center**
3. Then **Customize Controls**

From here, you decide what shows up and what doesn't. Like for example, if you're the type that doesn't use much of **flashlight**, you can remove and put something like **Voice memos** that you use regularly.

Force apps to close

There's no home button so you would think that you can't force quit stubborn apps. Actually think again. You can. Though it's a tad more complex than before.

1. Bring the **App Switcher** up. That means swiping up from the bottom corner of the screen
2. **Press** and **hold** the app you want to remove
3. Tap the **red minus** sign at the left corner of the screen.

It's usually believed that forcing apps to quit help to save battery. But actually apple says it does quite the opposite, it reduces the battery.

Some apps are just too stubborn, so when they start acting up, you can follow this method..

Taking screenshots

Are you finding it tricky to take screenshots on your iPhone X? Or do you think screenshots are just for the phone gurus. Trust me, you'll scream when you find out how easy it is to take a screenshot. It's like knife slicing through butter.

Press and hold the **Side Button** and **Volume Up** at the same time. You should hear the shutter sound to signify it's been shot. Try it.

It works right. Told you you'll scream.

Force Phone To Reset

During the course of using your phone there's no way it won't freeze at some point. When that happens, all you just do is reset the phone. What this means is that your phone will shut down and restart again.

To reset;
1. Press the volume up button and release it
2. Press the volume down button and release it
3. Hold the side button down.

After this, it should restart. Then you should see the apple symbol that shows up when the phone is turning on.

Shut off alarms with your face.

Have you ever tried to switch of your blaring alarm in the middle of the night just to find that the touch pad keeps ceasing. Well I know that feeling. It sucks and can be frustrating.

But the iPhone X does away with that problem because you can now shut down alarms with your face. Yup, you don't have to snooze.

Once that alarm starts its daily noise, just bring your phone to your face. Face ID should find your face. Once it finds it, it should please your ears and quiet the volume.

Speedy face ID unlock

If you've been using Face ID, then you know how it works to unlock you phone. You raise it and after Face ID unlocks the phone you swipe up. But do you know that's the slower method.

Yeah you can do it much faster. And it's really easy. All you do is raise and you swipe.

Yes you read right. Just raise and you swipe. The speed and accuracy of Face ID is so top-notch that all you need to do is swipe up as long as the true depth camera is in front of your face. You don't have to wait all year for the lock to open.

Access the apple pay easily

Okay, so now the home button has been discarded. How then do we bring up the apple pay on or phone? Easy. That's what I love about apple. They remove stuffs and replace with way cooler stuffs.

With Apple Pay, all you do is double click the side button on your iPhone X. Then you'll have to verify using Face ID. After verification, you can move on with your transaction.

Specify What Face ID unlocks

Face ID is really beneficial. You don't have to start pressing pins. You just bring the phone to your face and it unlocks the. But the Face ID is not only to unlock the phone. You can also use it to fill forms in Safari, purchase from the app store and verify apple pay.

But all these things could be overwhelming and you may feel weary wary about using Face ID for some stuffs. And there's a way to cancel where you don't want Face ID to function.

1. Go to **Settings**
2. Select **Face ID & Passcode**

From here you can toggle where exactly you want Face ID to work.

Enable One-Handed Mode.

I'm sure you must've taken your time to examine your iPhone X. And as you can see it's no small boy. It's got a very wide screen.

A time might come when you'll have to type singlehandedly. And I tell you that's no easy task. You start you feel pain in your hands and it's just nasty.

But you could say Apple saw this coming. They've provided the one-handed mode. What this does is it compresses the keyboard to be easily accessible by one hand.

To use this feature, hit the **emoji key icon** in the keyboard then choose either left or right handed keyboard and it will swish to a side.

Terminate Face ID Quickly.

If by chance you suddenly start to grow a hatred for the Face ID, you can turn it off. For example if you're in a place where you can be forced to look at your phone to unlock it.

As quick as you can, hit the side button five times. It should turn on Face ID immediately. After Face ID is off it will automatically switch to your passcode for you to unlock.

Easy Control Center Access

Reaching from top of your iPhone X top swipe down the control center with one is not exactly the most painless thing to do. But again Apple makes it easier with this setting called Reachability.

To access this;

1. Enter **Setting**
2. Then **General**
3. Select **Accessibility**
4. Then just below **interactions**, turn on **Reachability**

Now that **Reachability** is activated, all you do is swipe down on the **gesture bar** and the screen will move down so that you can be able to touch the top icons.

And it think is better. Less pain more gain.

Make your iPhone X Battery last a decade.

You know that's just an expression right. But there are tricks that you can use to make you go for about a day without needing to charge. In fact depending on how much you use. It can even last you for two days.

First of all, you want to put your phone in **low power mode**.

1. Got to **Settings**
2. Choose **Battery**
3. Then **low power mode**

Next,

1. Enter **Settings**
2. Select **General**
3. Then **Accessibility**
4. Choose **Display accommodations**.
5. Select **Color Filters** and toggle it on
6. Hit **Grayscale**.

Now still in **Display accommodations,**

1. Sclcct **invert colors**
2. Toggle on **classic invert**

Next you want to choose an all-white wallpaper. It will turn to all-black wallpaper since we've inverted the colors.

Activating Siri

Of course apple has to include Siri in the iPhone X. Siri is the virtual assistant that does what task is given by your voice command. There's a power button at the right side of your iPhone X. Press and hold it to activate Siri.

At the bottom of the screen, you should see the Siri listening sign on the screen. Once you see Siri, you release the button. You can now issue a voice command like "What time is it in Los Angeles?"

Taking Photo In The Portrait Mode.

Using portrait mode on the iPhone X can be very delightful. And you can even use it both on the front camera or the camera at the rear.

Open your camera app. Select portrait. Then you should see an array of Portrait lighting effect options. Like Studio light to brighten the features of the face, Stage light to separate the person in spotlight, Contour light to add directional light and others.

To switch to the front camera, hit the camera rotate icon.

Using Animoji

With the iPhone X you can be able to create an Animoji that mimics your facial expressions and voice and even share it with anyone.

To do this,

1. Open the **messages app** and make as if to start a conversation.
2. Hit the emoji icon
3. Select **Animoji**.
4. Put your face in the frame and start recording
5. You can preview your emoji by click the top corner by the left.
6. To change your Animoji, just choose another Animoji.
7. Choose **send**.

To save an Animoji

1. Open any message that the Animoji is in.
2. Tap and hold the Animoji.
3. Select **save**

Use One Tapping To Wake

I'm sure you know of the other android phones that uses double tap to wake. They've been kinda bragging about this for years now. But the iPhone X has that. In fact I doesn't have that, it has better. A wake feature that needs just one tap.

This feature is ever so nice if you're trying to do quick tasks like looking at notifications without much stress or checking the time. To use this nice feature, just tap any place on the phone's screen.

The Beauty Of Slow Sync Flash

Have you ever taken a picture in the dark? I know I have, using my phones flash as light. And belive me when I say the that you wouldn't want to try it again. The image can be really nasty.

But that's because the photo is taken at a high shutter speed. And low lighting and fast shutter speed doesn't work very well together.

But what now happens when the shutter speed is slow or with slow sync flash?. Well I shouldn't say much, try it yourself, you'll be amazed. You'll get a sweet image.

If you want to activate iPhone X slow sync flash, use the flash.

Chapter 5

Tips and Tricks for the iPhone XS

Using The Portrait Mode

Using portrait mode with your iPhone XS is so smooth and it even gets better as you can use it with either the front-facing camera or the camera at the rear.

Using portrait mode is walk in the park. All you do is enter the **Camera app** and slide left on the menu slider and you should see **Portrait**.

From here you should see options of different lighting. Like Contour light, Natural light, Stage light and others. If you want to use the front camera in portrait mode, just hit the **rotate camera symbol** beside the **shutter icon**.

Control Depth.

The Depth Control option is very new to the iPhone world and of course you guessed right, iPhone XS has this feature. What Depth Control does is that it enables you be able to control the amount of blur that's in the background of the photo that has been taken.

To use this feature,
1. Enter **Photos**
2. Choose a portrait mode photo
3. Click **Edit**

You should see a slider down that allows you to manipulate the blur to how you want.

Use The Memoji.

With the previous iPhone X, apple gave us the ability to create Animojis . But with this iPhone XS, they are topping it a notch with a feature called **Memoji**. They are available on the iOS 12 of iPhone XS.

What a Memoji does is that it controls animated avatars using your facial expressions

To create a Memoji,

1. Open **Messages**
2. Click the **app drawer**
3. Select the **monkey symbol**.

From here on, you will be able to customize your Memoji to your desire. After customizing and you are okay with it, save it by hitting **Done** at the top of the display.

Become Skilled At Using Gestures

Who knows may be the iPhone X is your first iPhone that does not have a home button. But fear not, you can learn how to use cool gestures to get by.

One of the gestures you can use is the swiping down from the bottom of the screen. When you do this, you can switch between apps easily. By swiping up, you will be able to shut down apps that you don't need any more.

You can also swipe down from the top. From the center, swipe down and the notifications will open. The **Control panel** appears when you swipe down from the right.

Enable Do Not Disturb.

You might just want to block out the noise one day and silence all notifications and calls. At that moment, what you do is switch **Do Not Disturb** on.

With **Do Not Disturb**, all notifications and calls are silent which is great as you can use it in the car so you don't get tempted to reply to a message. If you can't hear it, you can't answer it.

1. Go to **Settings**
2. Then **Do Not Disturb**
3. Toggle **Do Not Disturb** on

To still be able to receive calls from specific contacts, click the **Allow Calls From** and set your desired contact.

Bring back the home button

If you've just got the iPhone XS, I'm sure you've been wondering why on earth did they have to remove the home button. I've felt your pain but really you get used to it pretty quickly.

But if you are a diehard fan, I'm happy to tell you that there's a way you can get your home button back. Well of course not the physical hardware home button, I'm talking about the virtual one.

All you do is,
1. Go to **Settings**
2. Select **General**.
3. Tap **Accessibility**
4. Choose **Assistive Touch**

From here, you can specify shortcuts of single tap, long press.

Taking A Screenshot.

There's no home button and I'm sure you're used to clicking the home and power button to take screenshots. The question is; How is possible to take screenshots now with no home button on the iPhone X.

It's fairly easy to do. All you do is hold down the power button and the home button immediately. An image should show up at the bottom of the screen at the left side. And you can also hear the screenshot sound.

Enable True Tone.

There's this feature that's available on the iPhone X iOS 12. It is the true tone. What true tone does is that it adapts the color brightness of the screen to match the surroundings where you are. This helps to reduce the strain effect it will have on your eyes.

You should have this setting enabled on your phone by default, so you don't have to worry about switching anything on. But just in case, this option is for some reason not activated or you switched it off by mistake, Just go to **Settings** then **Display And Brightness**.

Face ID Security

Previously the security we had on our iPhones was Touch ID and we thought apple really made it. But with iOS 12 they've gone further. We now have Face ID.

And as the name implies, Face ID is an authentication process that relies on the information of the face for security.

To set Face ID up,

7. Enter **Settings app**
8. Select **Face ID and Passcode**.
9. Enter passcode.
10. Choose **Set up Face ID**
11. Follow the prompts it gives you and allow your face to be in the frame. Tilt your head slowly to finish the circle.
12. You will have to do it again. Follow the same steps.

Enable Siri on the iPhone XS

You know Siri right? The helpful Apple virtual assistant that carries out tasks according to what you command it. One of the tasks you can delegate to Siri is 'What is the time in London now? And the ever wise assistant will answer you.

To set up Siri.

1. Enter your **Settings**
2. Select **Siri & Search**
3. Then **Listen For 'Hey Siri'**
4. After this, To call up Siri, just say "Hey Siri"

Video Quality Like No Other

The video quality of your iPhone is set to 1080p by default. But who cares about default. There's a way you can set your phone to shoot videos with super high quality. And by high quality, I mean 4k resolution at 60 Fps (frames per second), incredible right? That's four times that of 1080p, imagine how smooth that can get.

To switch to 4k from the default 1080p,
1. Enter **Settings**
2. Move down and select **camera**
3. Hit **Record video**
4. Choose **4k at 60 fps**

Utilize Group FaceTime

In your iPhone XS, you can engage in group **FaceTime** calls. The number of people you can engage in with ranges up to 32. To set up group session, open the FaceTime app and manually choose whoever you want to add.

In fact, you can try it on a group chat in imessage and begin a FaceTime group call.
To do this

1. Open the **chat**
2. Click the initials that's at the top of the chat window.
3. Tap the camera symbol.

As the group FaceTime calls proceed, you can even add Animojis or stickers

Make Use Of One-Handed Mode

The iPhone XS is undeniably large. And it can be a real pain trying to navigate to type a message through the whole screen with one hand. Apple provided an antidote; they call it the one handed keyboard mode.

This feature is really awesome. What it does is it squishes the whole key board to one side, either left or right. With is this it's much easier typing messages with one hand.

Too let this feature be turned on all the time,

1. Go to **Settings**
2. Select **General**
3. Tap **keyboards**
4. Then **One-handed mode**
5. Choose between right or left.

But if don't want it to be on always, just click the emoji icon on the keyboard. Choose either left or right.

Split The Screen's View

So you've got this really big screen, it will be a big waste if you don't make use of it well. You can go on with the normal display of the phone or you could just split the screen. When you use the split view in your iPhone XS it makes you get an extra view of some apps

Using split view is easy. Just open an app or website that works with it and rotate your phone to landscape mode. Verify that rotation lock is off. If it is not, from the top right side of the screen, swipe down and unlock the rotation lock icon.

Turning Phone Off

We all know that the button at the side of the phone is usually the power button. Of course that's how it has always been. But not this time around with the iPhone XS. That button is the lock button. So a good question is; How do we turn our phones off then?

The answer is not farfetched. Just press and hold the **Volume down** button and the **Power button** immediately. Wait a little and the slider to turn off should show.

Set Up Apple Pay

Do you know that you can leave your wallet at home and pay for items with your iPhone? Yeah, and that is only made possible with Apple pay. With it, you can pay for items.

To use it, you'll first insert a card to the wallet by,
1. Going to **Settings**
2. Selecting **Wallet and Apple pay**
3. Then **Apple Pay**

Before you can use it, you should first contact your bank. It's very easy to use Apple Pay once it is set. Quickly press the lock button twice (lock button at the ride side of the phone). Scan your face if you set Face ID so purchase can be approved.

Access To Notification Center

What's interesting about the notification center is that you have access to it anywhere, anytime no matter what you're doing on your iPhone. Whether you're in an app or at homescreen or lockscreen

It's very easy to this. Just swipe down from the very top of the screen and the notification center should open. Though you want to be careful not to tap the right corner of the screen because that's where the control center is

Force Closing Apps

If you close an app on your iPhone XS the app still runs in the background. Some apps still perform certain tasks even though it is the background. To stop this we can force close the apps.

To force close an app,
1. Swipe up from the bottom of the screen
2. Don't release your hand, hold it for a while.
3. Now a card should appear, swipe up the card of the app you want to force close.

It is said though that force closing apps tends to drain more battery.

Customizing The Control Center

Customizing the control center is a cool option. It makes it easier to reach for features that you tend to use more often. You don't have to go far. You can even remove the ones that you think you don't need.

To do this,

4. Go to the **Settings**
5. Tap **Control Center**
6. Select **Customize Control**

Now you can remove and add what shows up on the control center, just tap the green (+) button to add a feature. A cool feature that you might want to add is the Apple TV remote.

Chapter 6

Tips And Tricks For iPhone XS Max

Start using Siri

On your iPhone XS Max, you have two ways to access Siri. Siri is Apple's virtual assistant and can be quite helpful. It can help you perform certain tasks or answer some questions you ask it.

One way to launch Siri is to

5. Go to **Settings**
6. Choose **Siri & Search**
7. Select '**Listen For 'Hey Siri'**'. Obey the instructions it tells you to do
8. From now, you can call Siri by saying "Hey Siri"

Another way is to press and hold the button at the side of the phone. Once you do this, Siri should show up.

Learn the Gestures

I'm sure you were a little taken aback when you saw that the iPhone XS Max comes without a home button. Believe me we were not expecting that. But apple has replaced that with features that I think are way cooler. And it only gets better with the fact that they are way too easy to navigate.

One of them is the swiping from the bottom of the display to gain access to the home screen. Another is swiping to the bottom of the screen to open the control center.

If you want to open recently used apps, just swipe up and make sure to hold for some time.

Extra muscle to Augmented Reality.

In your iPhone XS Max, you should see a measure app. This app is available to iOS 12 devices. What it does is, it uses your phones AR (Augmented Reality) potentials to give you a nice experience.

To make use of this, open up the app. You should see a plus button, press it and use it to make different points in the three dimensional surface. You can use this to measure full rectangles or single lines. To copy it, tap on a figure.

To take a photo of your measurements, use the shutter button.

Use Face ID

The home button is gone, but Apple has provided a sweet way to unlock our iPhones. It's called **Face ID**. What Face ID does is that it saves the information on your face and uses it to unlock your phone next time you show it.

You've got to set it up before you can use it. First make sure that you are in a place with good lighting. Then;

1. Go to **Settings**
2. Select **Face ID and Passcode**. If you don't have a Passcode, you'll be asked to create one.
3. Choose **Setup Face ID**
4. Next you'll have to scan your face two times. Follow the instructions it gives.
5. Now, when your phone is in lock screen, swipe up and put the phone to your face.

Taking screenshots

For those coming from old iPhones or Android, taking a screenshot on the iPhone XS Max can be a little confusing. Y'know, with the homescreen gone and all.

But it's fairly easy. Just hold down the volume up button and the power button together. After you do this, your phone will shine white and you should see a small screenshot thumbnail at the bottom corner of the screen. After taking screenshot, you can even edit it so as to crop out unwanted places.

Setting up apple pay

With your iPhone XS Max, apple makes life much easier with **Apple Pay**. With it, you can pay for items easily without bringing your wallet, all you need is your iPhone. To use Apple Pay, you've got to add your card to the wallet

4. Enter **Settings**
5. Choose **Wallet and Apple pay**
6. Select **Apple Pay**

It's really simple to use Apple Pay after it is set. Hit the lock button quickly at the right side of the phone two times. If Face ID is set, scan your face to approve purchase.

Measure screen time

With your mighty iPhone XS Max, Apple makes sure you can measure your screen time so that you are not making use of your phone more than you should. It's not that hard to find the screen time tracker, just go in the **Settings** and select **Screen Time** utility.

With screen time utility, you can track how much you are using your phone and also find out t what apps are using up your valuable time. This will enable you to be able to set limits.

Use portrait mode

Have you ever seen he wonders of the portrait mode in action before? It's just flat out beautiful. And with the iPhone XS Max, you can shoot in portrait mode with the front facing camera and the camera at the rear.

If you want to use portrait mode and witness it's abilities,

1. Open your camera app
2. Slide left on the menu slider. Stop when you see portrait
3. You should also see different lighting options like, Contour light, Natural light, Stage light. Choose lighting setup you wish
4. Hit shutter to take a picture. TO use to front camera, press the camera rotate symbol.

Using the depth control

Controlling the depth is a new option for the iPhones and sure the iPhone XS Max has it too. What depth control does is that, it enables you to control the blur that is the back ground of the in image even though you've already taken the photo.

To arm yourself with the depth control feature, just select the photo and you want to tweak, choose edit. The slider for depth control should show up now. Shift it to your heart's desire.

Create a Memoji

Apple's new iPhone XS Max allows you to create your Memoji without stress. In their previous phones, Apple released the Animoji and we were all thrilled. That came with the iPhone X.

But now what we have is Memoji. This Memoji enables user to make their own animated avatars. You can even control this avatar with your facial expressions.

To create a Memoji, all you have to do is
1. Open the **Message app** on your phone.
2. Click the **Appstore** symbol
3. Then the **small monkey** symbol
4. Select the **plus button** to **start**.

From here you can customize your face, hair color, skin and more. Once you're through with creating, hit **Done**

Turning Off Your Phone.

With the new iPhone XS Max, a task as simple as turning off the phone can be a real issue if you don't know what to do. Previously we all know that he button at the right side of the phone was the power button, but now since the side button is to launch Siri now, the question is, 'how I switch my phone off.

Piece of cake. Just press and hold the **volume down** or **up button** with the **side lock button** together at the same time. It should not take long before you see the option turn off your phone.

Switch On The True Tone Display

With the iPhone XS Max you have the true taste of the world's latest advancement in technology. And one of the improvements is the **True Tone**. This is the ability for your phone's screen to shift its color and temperature to adjust to the location you're in.

To enable **True Tone**, all you do is
   1. Enter the **Settings**.
   2. Choose **Display and Brightness**.
   3. From here, toggle on **True Tone**

Using Memoji On FaceTime Calls

Memojis are fun use and can really spice up your conversations. With your iPhone XS Max, you can use both Memoji and Animoji in group calls or in one-on-one calls. You might be wondering how to do it?

1. Open the Face Time app on your phone. Start a call.
2. You should see a rectangular inlay that is at the bottom of the display, tap it
3. Select the Animoji symbol.
4. From here you have access to any Memoji that you've made and Animojis. Choose the one that you desire

Own Your Notifications

You know those entirely pointless notifications that make blaring noises and fill up your lock screen display? Yes those ones. You can have a lot more control over them now than before.

By control I mean you can quiet them down so that they go easy on your ears. Or so that they just go to the notification center peacefully. They don't have to appear on your lock screen, make noise and start to pop as a banner.

To be able to this;

1. Press and hold a notification as it comes and appears on the screen.
2. Select **Manage**
3. Choose **Deliver Quietly**.

Enable Display Zoom

Display zoom is a feature on the iPhone XS Max that makes whatever is on the screen of your phone to be a higher resolution. When this happens, the contents are a lot easier to read.

To switch on display zoom;

1. Enter **Settings**
2. Then **Brightness and View**
3. Choose **Display zoom**.
4. From here you can choose either **standard view** or **zoomed view**. There's a preview to show the differences between the two
5. Click on the one you desire. Your phone should restart for the resolution to change.

What **zoomed** does is that is shows you the same content but on a bigger display.

Enabling Do Not Disturb

Everyone wants themselves some quiet and peaceful time, free of disturbances. Maybe you're in your car and you want to avoid ringing from notifications or calls. You don't have to switch your phone off, all you do is turn on **Do Not Disturb**.

1. Enter **Settings**
2. Select **Do Not Disturb**.
3. Switch on the toggle beside **Do Not Disturb**

To state clearly who to accept calls from, select the **Allow Calls From** and specify your desired contact. With this option, you will only get calls from the people you wish.

Split The View

IPhone XS Max, the biggest iPhone in history. You have this extra screen space and it's just mindboggling to let all the extra screen space just go to waste. You can split the view of the phone to get extended view of apps

There are many apps that work with split view, certain websites too. Like the **New York Times**. With the **Mail app**, you get to see an extra preview screen along with your normal current view

To use the split view, you want to swipe down from the top right of the display and unlock the rotation lock sign. Now open an app. As long as the website or app is compatible with split screen, it should work.

Switch To One-Handed Mode

Since you've gotten your 6-inch iPhone XS Max, have you tried to navigate the screen and type messages using only one hand? If you have then you'll understand what I'm talking about. It can cause some serious hand ache.

But to relive the pain, Apple as provided the One-Handed mode that makes the keyboard squeeze either to the right or to the left.

To enable One-Handed mode,
1. Go to **Settings**
2. Select **General**
3. Then **Keyboards**
4. Choose **One-Handed keyboard**

That will make it to be switched on all the time you want to type a message.

If you don't want it to be on always, you can just;
1. Go to iMessage.
2. When the keyboard is open, press and hold the emoji key that is on the left corner of the screen and select either the right side or left side keyboard
3. To turn it off, press and hold the icon like before and chose middle keyboard

Rescue Your Home Button.

As must have noticed, the home button of the iPhone XS Max has been thrown out to the garbage. And for old users of iPhone who decided to get the iPhone XS Max for liberation, it can be a bit confusing to cope and learn all the gestures.

There's no problem, we just gather our army and get the home button back. Of course you now it's not the physical home button, we are getting a virtual one. Well at least it's something.

To enable the home button,
1. Fire up the **Settings app**
2. Enter **General**
3. Move to **Accessibility**
4. Select **Assistive touch**.

Chapter 7

How To Use Apple Pay

It is now ever easy to use Apple pay. It can even be done through the iMessage app. All you do to activate is place the top of your phone near the **NFC** card terminal while putting your finger on the iPhone's sensor for Touch ID. But to be able to perform all these wonders, you've got set Apple pay up first.

Setting Up The Apple Pay

1. Open **Wallet**
2. Select **Add Credit or Debit card**.
3. Put your card details. Your card will now be verified with your bank
4. Once that is done, you are able to use Apple Pay.

Using The Apple Pay.

1. Put your phone near the card reader and what will appear on the screen should be the image of your card.

2. If you use Touch ID, Place your finger on the Touch ID sensor. Once your fingerprint is confirmed, you're golden.

If you want another card, press the one that is on the screen and select a different card. Real simple, uh?

However if your phone uses Face ID like iPhone X and higher, the process is a little different. It's not hard though. You just click twice on the side button. Then put your face to the camera so it can scan your face. After this, you simply hold the phone toward the card reader. Double click the side button again, if you want to use another card and just select a different card.

Chapter 8

Tips for using iOS 12 effectively

Saving Your Passwords

In the iOS 12 there a totally cool feature that helps users be able to follow up on their passwords. The new iOS is armed with a feature called **AutoFill Passwords**. This is usually kept in the iCloud keychain.

With this, you can add your own username and passwords from your **Settings app** to set for only some apps and websites. This feature will fill in your information automatically for you once you use Face ID or Touch ID after it identifies the ones that are logged

Ability To Turn On 'Do Not Disturb' During Bedtime.

The **Do Not Disturb** option got totally revamped in the iOS 12. With its extra feature, you are able to customize it more to suit your taste. Not only can you state clearly what times you want **Do Not Disturb** to be on at day, you can even set it to Bedtime mode.

If you set it, this will quiet down all the notifications all the way till the morning. To let you know that it the feature is set, the screen will display just the date and time and become dim.

Measuring Objects With An App.

Using the camera of your iPhone, iOS 12 allows you to measure objects with AR. When you use the measure app, you'll be able to measure different objects.

All you do is,

1. Open the **Measure app**.
2. Fix your iPhone's camera on the object to measure
3. Follow the guides it gives to line up your phone correctly.
4. Next, to view the measurements, you just click the display

Every display will always show the option to switch form inches to centimeters. Of course it doesn't give an accurate measurement like a hardware tape rule, it is really handy if you just want to take a quick measurement of an item.

Insert Siri shortcuts

There's a new advancement with Siri in the iOS 12. It's the option to add immediate actions and shortcut to Siri. Thought this option is still in beta for now and you can't do plenty with it, there are still some perks you can enjoy.

Like how you can set a voice commands so that Siri can do some specific tasks. Example, **View New photos.**
If you want to set a voice command'
1. Enter your **Settings**.
2. Selects **Siri and Search**
3. Click **My Shortcuts**

Once that is open you will be able select anyone that Siri suggests.

Track your screen time

In the iOS 12, apple is trying to urge us to use our phones lesser so we can have time for other important activities. There's this new feature, **Screen time**.

Screen time is an opportunity for you to set Downtime, check your phone usage and find out which apps are really eating away your time. When you use down time, you are able to put away your phone by restraining some applications from forwarding notifications.

Place Limits on apps

This is also one of the perks of screen time. It enables you to set app limits. This will enable you to reduce the time you spend on certain apps. You will be able to set how long the ban should last and for which days.

If you want to set app limits.
1. Fire up the **Settings app**
2. Move to **Screen time**
3. Then **App limits**. Select the groups of apps you want to set limit. Click the **Add**

Easy Force Closing apps.

With the iOS 12, the process of force closing apps is a lot simpler. Not only simpler also quicker. All you do is swipe up from the bottom of the display and just start swiping the apps you want to quit like that.

Y'know, previously force closing apps on phones without home button on previous iOS will have to take a longer method. You'll have to swipe up and hold down and wait before a minus sign will appear, then you now click

But now with newer phones like the iPhone XS and XS Max, they all have the iOS 12, so the process is a lot simpler.

Chapter 9

How To Use Siri On Your Iphone

Siri is the ever helpful apple voice assistant that you dish out commands to on your iPhone and it just it just carries it out for you.

But something to note is that there's not a specific app icon for Siri that you just tap and it open. So how then do you access Siri. For newer generations of iPhones, accessing Siri can be a little confusing even if you have been using previous versions of iPhone. All of that we will cover here

How to invoke Siri

By Clicking the home button or side button

On older versions of iPhone, pressing and holing the home button on your device will call up Siri. But on the iPhone X and higher, you summon Siri by pressing the button at the side of the phone.

By using the Bluetooth headset button.

If you use a headset that has remote, press and hold the button at the center and you should hear a ding.

By saying hey Siri

If your iPhone is iOS 8 or higher, you can summon Siri hands free by saying 'Hey Siri'. But you've got to first set it up.

1. Got to **Settings**
2. Choose **Siri & Search**
3. Enable **Listen For 'Hey Siri'** and obey the prompts it provides
4. From now you can summon Siri without having to press anything just say **"Hey Siri"**

What Can Siri do for you,

- Send messages for you
- Set a timer for you
- Play music
- Send tweets
- Check the weather
- Schedule events
- Send emails
- Calculate
- Find locations

Here are some things you can ask Siri

- 'Hey Siri, Set an alarm for 6 am'
- 'Hey Siri, What is the time New York?'
- 'Hey Siri, schedule a meeting with Sarah for Tuesday at 11oclock
- 'Hey Siri, how cold will it be today?'
- 'Hey Siri, remind me to do the dishes?'
- 'Hey Siri, play me Roar by Katy Perry'
- 'Hey Siri, call David Randall
- 'Hey Siri, open the Settings App'
- 'Hey Siri, how do I say hello in Spanish?'
- 'Hey Siri, who is the President of Iceland?'
- 'Hey Siri, turn off Bluetooth'

How to type and ask Siri

If you're the type that doesn't really fancy talking to Siri, you don't have to say something. You can just type your command. Though you'll have to set it up first

Here's how.

1. Enter **Settings**
2. Go to **General**
3. Select **Accessibility**
4. Move down to Siri and click the line

5. Switch on **Type To Siri**

6. The next time you activate Siri, all you do is type in your command

Tips To Ensure That Siri Serves You Well

While the apples virtual assistant is known for its top notch abilities, you may encounter some problems with it. Implement these few tips to allow Siri to better

Control how long Siri will listen

You have the power to control how long Siri will continue to encode your commands. You don't have to wait for it to recognize that you have stopped talking.

Just make sure that while you're asking your question or saying your command, you're holding down the power button

Alter Siri's language.

One of the key reasons why Siri may not understand your commands well can be because of your language. Even in English. Let's say you speak UK English. Siri may misinterpret your commands. So what you want to do is set the English to 'English (United Kingdom)

To adjust the language,

1. Enter the **Settings**
2. Go to **Siri and Search**
3. Select Language
4. Choose your desired language.

Having Smooth Data Connection

If you don't have data connection, Siri won't work. How Siri functions is that it records your voice and sends it to a server which converts your sayings and gives it back as text.

So if you're not connected to the internet, Siri is not going to work.

Changing Siri's gender

If you're a male and you prefer to have a male virtual brother around, you can switch the gender. Same goes for females.

Just,

1. Enter **Settings**
2. Then **Siri and Search**
3. Choose **Siri Voice**

4. Select your preferred voice.

Chapter 10

How To Maintain Your iPhone

We all know that iPhones are not biscuit change. They cost high. Well, they give superb quality so they are very well worth it. But such an investment will go to total waste if you don't take proper care of your treasure.

So here are some iOS maintenance tips for your consumption.

Put The Unwanted In The Garbage Truck

Do you remember that game that your buddy told you to try out and you felt it was total trash? Or yes, that app your neighbor introduced to you only for to find that it was a complete waste of time. Yes those applications. I'm pretty sure they are still sitting there in you app list

Throw them out and send them packing immediately. Not only do they use up the space of the phone, they also make it sluggish and your device slow. To delete an app, press and hold the app until it shakes like it's waving 'hey look at me' and delete or press the X at the corner.

Back Them Up

It's funny how many people do the bad stuff and only few do the good, like backing up your iPhones. You need to train yourself so that it becomes a habit.

Reason why backing up is so essential is because of this. Let's say your iPhone gets missing (I really hope that doesn't happen) or you there was a software update gone wrong or your device becomes faulty, retrieving your files will be almost impossible.

So don't wait for me, just back your phone up. You can back your phone up with iCloud or iTunes. In fact what's stopping you, just do both!

Update iOS

You be like 'Who needs an update. My iOS is just fine'. And I want you discard that feeling and throw it far away.

You need an update. With every new iOS there are fixes to bugs, updates for security, and brand new features and perks. You stick to your old iOS and it will be like you're living in the Stone Age.

What more, updating is like the easiest thing to do. Since we have OTA (Over The Air), updating iOS is just a matter of minutes.

To update,

1. Make sure to back up your phone as we warned earlier
2. Enter **Settings**
3. Then **General**
4. Then Choose **Software update**.
5. If an update is available, click **Download and install**.

Phone case and Screen protector

We all know how phone cases and screen protectors saves our lives every once in a while. Okay, not our life per say, it's our phones. Whenever your phone drops, a protective phone case will help to absorb the effect and shock of the fall.

And screens, oh screens are really special. And believe me when I say that you do not want them to break. So just buy a screen protector.

When you're purchasing either of the two, make sure it's of good quality and the design is what you desire.

Chapter 11

Prolonging Your iPhones Battery Life.

As with maintenance of phones, we all know how much battery means to us. Check out these tips to extend your phones battery life.

Forget Quitting Apps

You may probably be doing this, quitting apps regularly, I usually do so too in the past. But stop. You might think that you're saving you're battery, but actually you're degrading it.

In 2014, Apple explained to us that quitting apps sucks more battery as the next time you want to open the app, it will start all over again thereby, eating the batter.

Using The Auto Brightness Option.

Using full screen brightness sucks away your battery and I'm sure you know that. Unless you really need the extra brightness, don't be stubborn just use auto brightness.

This adjusts the screens brightness to the surroundings you're in.

Turn Low Power Mode On

Normally when you're phone reaches 20%, you'll be prompted to switch to low power mode. But you don't have to wait for your phone to urge you before you switch it. You can do it right after you finishing charging.

Low power mode stops all the background tasks and gives you more battery.

Turn Off Bluetooth.

It's not a new thing that putting your Bluetooth on regularly reduces the battery life. So if you're not using the Bluetooth, just put it off

Chapter 12

Apple Watch Tips And Tricks

Get Into The Control And Notification Center Easily

There was a time when the only way you could get into the Notification Center and Control Center was through the face screen of the watch. However with the recent watchOS you have the ability to access the Control Center and Notification Center from just about anywhere. With this, you can even access them from Third-party apps

What you do is put your finger at the top or bottom of the watch display. You should now see a piece of the Control Center or the notification center. Once it shows, you now have the ability to expand it to full display.

Say Bye To Walkie-Talkie

Any time you raise your wrist, there's a chance that you'll see a Walkie-Talkie icon that comes out at the top of the screen. If this is this case, then we could say that you've checked yourself in the Walkie-Talkie app as available.

If you would like to remove this relentless symbol,
1. Open up the **Walkie-Talkie app** on the Apple Watch
2. Then you go upwards to the top of contacts. You do this by using the digital crown of the watch.
3. Tap and turn off **Available**

Immobilize Notifications

There are things set by default on your watch. And one of them is the fact that your watch brings up the notifications from apps on your iPhone with alerts. At first you might think this is cool, but it might get old very fast.

To turn it off, just
1. Wait for the time you receive a notification from an app that you want to disable the notifications for.
2. When it shows up, slide left from it.
3. From here you should see three dots, select it
4. Choose **Turn Off On Apple watch**

This option to disable is really cool cause in previous watchOS, you would have to dig in your iPhone app and enter each app one by one to disable them.

Offline Podcast

Apple has finally launched the longed-for app for Podcasts. This is available in watchOS 5 and it allows you to use your iPhone to stream podcasts. You can do this with cellular data or Wi-Fi. Then you can be able to listen to them through headphones that are connected to Bluetooth

But something that is interesting is, with this Podcast app, you can sync and keep current podcasts for your iPhone straight to you Apple watch. With this you can now listen you them offline. To find the list of episodes, go to **Library** then select **Episodes**.

Use A Monogram

If you're one who uses the Infograph watch face or Color watch face then you would like to hear that you can now add a custom monogram. This can be used to form your initials, nickname and others.

If you would like to make your own monogram,
1. Open the **iPhone Watch App**
2. Choose **My Watch** tab
3. Hit **Clock**
4. Select **Monogram**

Include some letters in the field. With this, when next you choose the info graph watch face or Color watch face, you can select Monogram.

Tweak The Design Of The Control Center

With the watchOS 5 you can now change the buttons in the Control Center to the way you want. Previously, the Control center design was permanent.

To do this;
1. Enter the **Control Center** normally
2. Move to the bottom and chose **Edit**
3. To show that they are set for you to move them, the buttons should start to shake
4. Long press a button and move to the place it you want it to be

Connecting to a Wi-Fi

It has now been made possible to log in and browse Wi-Fi networks just from your own Apple watch. This feature is available on the watchOS 5. Previously, this was connected to the Wi-Fi of your iPhone.

To connect to a Wi-Fi network on your watch,
1. Enter the **Settings** app
2. Select **Wi-Fi**
3. From the list presented, choose a network that's available
4. From here you use the gesture input of the screen to enter the password

Include Cities In The Weather App.

Unlike any feature, the weather app has taken a complete overhaul in the watchOS 5 since the previous versions. When you select the radial forecast for one city, it will round up through chance of rain, temperature and other conditions

Now, when you scroll down with the help of the digital crown, you will be able to get extra information like the speed of the wind or the air quality.

Also, you can also add further forecasts for different locations in the world.

1. In the main screen, scroll to the bottom
2. Select **Add City**
3. You can state your preference or just jot down the city name

Force-Quit Stubborn Apps

If this hasn't happened to you yet then it might still happen in the future. Some apps will just crash and stop refreshing and receiving live data. With the watch face complications, this can happen too.

When this happens all you is force-quit the app in your watch. To do this;

1. With the app you want to force-quit, hold down the side button of you Apple Watch
2. When the power down menu shows up, release the side button.
3. Now, hold down the Digital Crown

The app should quit and come back to the home screen so you can open it again

Talk To Siri With No Buttons

With the new watchOS, watchOS 5, you now have the feature of speaking to Siri on your watch without pressing the Digital crown. This option is very easy to use, you can find it in Settings.

1. Go to **Settings**
2. Then **General**
3. Select **Siri**
4. Choose **Raise To Speak**

When you've enabled this feature, all you have to do next time you want to invoke Siri, is to just raise your hand to your mouth and start to talk Siri.

Hey you don't even have to say 'Hey Siri'. Just start speaking.

Alert For Running Pace

For runners, this is good news. Apple has now made it possible for your apple watch to enable pace alerts. With this you be able to test your capability to stick to the set pace.

When you want to track your run next time,
1. Enter the **Workout App**
2. Select the button with three dots.
3. Slide to the bottom and hit **Set Pace Alerts**.

You can choose to get alerts for you average pace after you complete a mile.

Do The Activity Challenge

You may be someone who shares his activity with friends who use Apple Watches. Now you can do a 7-day activity competition with them and challenge them for the chance to win an award

To do this;
1. Enter the **Activity App** on your watch
2. Slide to the Sharing screen
3. Select a friend
4. Move down to the bottom and press the button for **Invite**

The invitation for the competition will be sent and the receiver will be given a deadline of 48 hours to reply.

Switch To Grayscale

On the Apple watch Series 4, the infograph watch faces can be really colourful especially when you've crammed them with complications. While this might be cool for some, for others it's just too much color. If you find the colorful display a little too much, you can always switch to grayscale.

To switch on the display setting to grayscale in the Apple Watch,

1. Enter the **My Watch** tab
2. Go to **General**
3. Then **Accessibility**
4. From here, turn on the toggle for **Grayscale**.

Quietly Get Notifications

To access this feature, all you do is go back to the same menu for notification management that we mentioned earlier. After you enabled this option, you can still get notifications from the application in question. The only thing is that you don't receive alerts as they are being sent to your Apple Watch

Something you should keep in mind is that these changes will be effective on your iPhone too. So this means that when those apps send notifications, you will still get them in your notification center. But they won't be all up in your face and start appearing on the lock screen, showing as a banner or making noises.

Browse And Clear

Apple has included the ability to support WebKit in the watchOS 5. What this is trying to say is that you can open web links that are gotten in apps on your watch. Like the links you get in Messages or Mail. With is feature, those contents don't have to pass you by, you can view them right from your watch.

If you would like to keep your browsing record private, the watchOS 5 also has the alternative to sweep the browsing history and any trace that your watch viewed that content.

All you do is;
1. Go to **Settings**
2. Then **General**
3. Select **Website Data**
4. Choose **Clear Website Data**

Setting Alarm

When you hear the term 'set alarm' on your watch, it sounds pretty easy to do, it's a watch how hard can setting alarm be. If you thought that, you're right. Setting alarms on your Alarms on your apple watch is not that hard. You just tell Siri something like; 'Set an alarm for 5 am'

But there's much more to do than just setting alarms. Like how to use Nightstand mode or how to set alarms and keep them silent.

To setup nightstand mode;
1. Enter the **Settings**
2. Then **General**
3. Select **Nightstand mode**

How To Take A Screenshot.

On your Apple watch, taking a screenshot is pretty easy. Just press the Digital crown and Action button simultaneously. Once you do that the image will now be saved in your iPhone's camera roll

This simple step to take a screenshot however does not happen by default. You'll have to switch on this option yourself.

1. Got to the **Watch Companion app**
2. Then **General**
3. From here you will be able to turn on and turn off **Enable Screenshots**

Adding Music To Your Watch

With cellular support, Apple music streaming is available directly on the Apple Watch. You still have the option to add mp3 music and connect it to Air Pods

To enable this,
1. Go to the **Companion Watch App**
2. Enter the **Music** Section
3. From here you can choose from the option it gives

Those options are a lot easier than before when you had to first create a playlist before you can sync any music.
If you want to get the best of your music, you will want to pair it with Bluetooth headphones. The watch will even ask you to if you would like to sync to headphones.

Use Your Watch To Unlock Your Mac

If you have a Mac to match with your Apple Watch, you can leave out passwords and use your watch to unlock your Mac. Just be sure that your Mac is using macOS Sierra 10.12 and newer or mid-2013

To pair these two devices together, you want to ensure that they are signed into your own iCloud account.

1. Go to **System Preferences** in you Mac
2. Choose **Security and Privacy**
3. Press the **General** tab
4. From here, you'll be able to set your Mac to be unlock by you watch

Verify that two-factor authentication is enabled on your Mac.

Alter The Volume Of The Air Pods

You have you ask Siri if you want to change the volumes on your Air Pods and not bring out your iPhone,
If you're using an Apple watch too you can also do something like that.

If you're playing music on your watch and it uses watchOS 5, you can change the volume by turning the Digital Crown. This is way is also convenient.

Using The Flashlight

Apple watch has a built in flashlight. To use it, just swipe up to open the Control Center and Select the Flashlight. You also have the option to even switch the light modes from flashing white to plain white to emergency red.

Use Your iPhone To Answer Watch Calls

If you have your iPhone with you, you can receive calls with your watch. Just make sure not to talk for a long time with it.

Whenever you get a call, Scroll up select **Answer on iPhone**.

Change The Size Of Texts

If you're one who strains to see what the notifications on the watch, you can just easily change the size of the texts.

To do this,

1. Go to **Settings**
2. Select **Brightness and Text Size**
3. Tweak it to how you see fit

Disclaimer

In as much as the author believes beginners will find this book helpful in learning how to use the iPhone 8, X, XS and XS Max, it is only a small book. It should not be relied upon solely for all iPhone tricks and troubleshooting.

About the author

Stephen Rock has been a certified apps developer and tech researcher for more than12 years. Some of his 'how to' guides have appeared in a handful of international journals and tech blogs. He loves rabbits.

Facebook page @ Techgist

www.ingramcontent.com/pod-product-compliance
Lightning Source LLC
Chambersburg PA
CBHW031240050326
40690CB00007B/883